# Aboriginal Canadian Communities
# SALISH
# COMMUNITY

BY M. M. EBOCH

True North is published by Beech Street Books
27 Stewart Rd. Collingwood, ON Canada L9Y 4M7

www.beechstreetbooks.ca

Produced by Red Line Editorial

Photographs ©: Corbis, cover, 1; Vancouver 125 - The City of Vancouver CC2.0, 4–5, 7, 16–17; Caelie_Frampton CC2.0, 8–9; William James Topley/Library and Archives Canada/PA-009555, 11; John Harper/Simon Fraser University CC2.0, 12–13; Edward S. Curtis/Library of Congress, 14; John W. Liston/Great Falls Tribune/AP Images, 18; Peter Gordon/CC2.0, 20; Red Line Editorial, 21

Editor: Amanda Lanser
Designer: Laura Polzin
Content Consultant: Dr. Bruce Granville Miller, Department of Anthropology, University of British Columbia

**Library and Archives Canada Cataloguing in Publication**

Eboch, M. M., author
    Salish community / by M.M. Eboch.

 (Aboriginal Canadian communities)
Includes bibliographical references and index.
Issued in print and electronic formats.
ISBN 978-1-77308-005-5 (hardback).--ISBN 978-1-77308-033-8 (paperback).--
ISBN 978-1-77308-061-1 (pdf).--ISBN 978-1-77308-089-5 (html)

    1. Salish Indians--Juvenile literature.  2. Salish Indians--Social life and customs--Juvenile literature.  3. Salish Indians--History--Juvenile literature. I. Title.

E99.S2E26 2016          j971.004'979435          C2016-903130-6
                                                 C2016-903131-4

Printed in the United States of America
Mankato, MN
August 2016

# TABLE OF CONTENTS

Chapter One

# LIVING BY WATER

T he Salish are a group of First Nations communities. The Salish live in the southwest region of Canada and northwest United States. Communities are often grouped as Coast or Interior Salish. Coast Salish live along the Salish Sea and the Fraser River. Interior Salish also live in British Columbia. Today, most Salish speak English. Some speak their **traditional** languages.

The **ancestors** of modern Salish lived in groups of up to 1,000 people. Many Salish communities were wealthy. This was especially true along the coast. Salish communities managed salmon fishing in the Fraser River. They built homes and equipment from cedar trees in the large forests. Communities had strong bonds with their neighbours. Conflicts were often resolved peacefully.

Salish musicians share their heritage with the public in Vancouver.

**SAY IT**

**qó:** (KOH): water

Europeans first came to Salish waters in 1790. At first, the Spanish came to trade. The Salish traded with and trapped for them. But disease had also come to the area with them. Many Salish got sick and died. But the number of Spanish and other Europeans kept growing.

## COAST SALISH COMMUNITIES

Strong Coast Salish families controlled hunting and fishing in their villages. They decided who owned houses and other property. Each Coast Salish village included several **longhouses**. Several families lived in each longhouse. Everyone lived in the same large room. Mats hung from the roof to divide the family areas. Each family area had its own fire pit. Food was stored in a hole dug in the dirt floor of the longhouse. This kept the food cool. Fish were hung from the ceiling.

All houses were built near water. Coast Salish painted the front of their houses bright colours. Each house had a carved interior **totem pole** or plank. The carvings portrayed a family's history and stories.

## INTERIOR SALISH COMMUNITIES

Each Interior Salish village had several leaders. Most were men known for their hunting and fishing skills. Interior Salish lived in pit houses. They dug a large, deep pit in the ground. A cone-shaped roof went over the hole. Earth and grass piled on the roof kept the room below warm. People entered the house by climbing down a ladder from the roof.

Salish communities teach their children their native languages and cultures.

In the summer, Interior Salish moved to find food. Men and women spent time by rivers to fish for salmon. Then they moved elsewhere to find ripe berries. They built movable camps for these trips. Their tents were made from woven mats hung on long sticks.

## SALISH COMMUNITIES TODAY

Today Salish people live in Canada and the United States. Some Salish remain on **reserves**. Others live in cities and towns. Expanding cities threaten Salish land. Some Salish work to protect their land and water rights.

# Chapter Two

# AT SCHOOL AND WORK

**S**alish children spend their childhoods learning. Before the 1800s, children did not go to school. Their parents taught them important life skills. Children lived with their extended families. They learned to respect their older family members. The head of the household was an especially influential person.

## FORCED TO CHANGE

British Columbia became part of Canada in 1871. Five years later, the Canadian government passed the Indian Act. It dramatically changed life for First Nations communities. The Canadian government wanted Salish and other **Aboriginal** Peoples to forget their traditions and **cultures**.

Many Salish children were sent to live at residential schools. Students were not allowed to speak their native languages.

Children in Salish communities learn skills from older family members.

Their education did not include their community's culture or history. Many First Nations children were forced to attend these schools. Some schools remained open until 1996. The Canadian government has admitted the schools hurt First Nations communities. The Prime Minister apologized to all former students in 2008. First Nations people received money to pay for the harm the schools had caused.

## SCHOOL TODAY

Today, most children attend their local schools. In a few cases, reserves also have their own schools. Students learn about First Nations cultures. Reserve schools teach students the traditions, arts, language, and history of their specific communities.

Several colleges offer special programs for Aboriginal people. These programs help students do well in college. Students study business, fine arts, education, science, and many other subjects. Other programs help First Nations students find jobs.

## WORKING SALISH

In the past, women made clothes out of animal skins and the soft inside of cedar bark. **Pigment** gave clothing color. Women wove mats out of cedar bark or rushes. They spun twine to make fishing nets and fishing lines. They wove baskets so tightly they could hold water. Salish men and women today continue to weave in traditional ways.

Canneries stole Salish communities' fishing rights, including those along the Fraser River.

In the late 1800s, many Salish worked in fish **canneries**. European men owned the canneries. They were likely built on land stolen from Coast Salish communities. Men, women, and children worked for the canneries. Few Salish fishers had the right to make money fishing on their own. Even traditional ways of fishing were banned in some areas. Restrictions on fishing lasted until 1984. That year, the Musqueam community of Coast Salish challenged the laws. They recovered their right to fish for food.

Today, some Salish make a living from the land and water. They work with people in government to make sure there will always be enough fish. But many others hold all types of jobs. They work as artists, lawyers, and teachers. Some Salish work for governments on reserves.

# Chapter Three

# EATING OFF THE LAND

Salish communities managed their lands and waters expertly. Men and women worked together. They gathered dozens of different plants, fruits, and berries. They grew **camas** for their edible roots. Men and women hunted and fished. They developed clam gardens on beaches. With care and attention, these areas were very productive.

Salish women did the cooking. They heated rocks in a fire. They filled a basket or wooden box with water. The hot rocks went into the basket or box. This made the water boil and cook the food. Women also baked and steamed food. They dried food to keep over winter. They served meals on wooden trays.

Salish communities created clam farms, similar to this one along the Broughton Archipelago.

Canoes made it easy for Salish people to get around, hunt, and trade.

# HUNTING AND FISHING

Men made tools out of bone, stone, and wood. Stone or shell blades could cut wood. They also used stone hammers and wooden wedges. With these tools, they cut trees for canoes.

Salish people used canoes for fishing and travel. Some canoes were up to 15 metres long. They could hold 50 people and 4,500 kilograms of fish. Men cut down a tall cedar tree. Then, they split the log in half. They burned and scraped out the middle of the trunk. Then they filled the hole with water and put in hot rocks. The water began to boil. The boiling water made the wood soft enough to carve.

In the canoes, men travelled along rivers and went out to sea. They fished for many kinds of fish, shellfish, and sea mammals. But salmon and herring were especially important. They are still important today.

Fishermen used several methods to catch fish. They fished with baited hooks on lines. Nets and traps gathered many fish in streams. But Salish men also had many animals to hunt. Deer, elk, and bear were common targets. Hunters used bows and arrows or traps. Nets caught birds. Harpoons and spears killed seals and whales.

# KEEPING THE PAST ALIVE

Later, Europeans brought iron tools and guns. The Salish traded with the Europeans and started using these items. These tools made cooking and hunting easier and faster. Today some Salish hunt and fish in traditional ways. Others use modern guns and fishing poles.

Many modern Salish enjoy traditional foods. Some learn traditional cooking at home. Others take classes. Community centres teach people how to catch, clean, and smoke fish the old way. Modern Salish people also learn to do bead work, make drums, or weave cedar baskets.

Chapter Four

# CELEBRATE!

Each Salish community had its own spiritual beliefs and rituals. Spirit dancing was an important ritual in Coast Salish communities. Special spiritual leaders called shamans helped guide people. They treated the sick. Most shamans were men, but women could also be shamans.

Starting in the 1800s, European **missionaries** visited the Salish. They wanted the Salish to become Christians. Canadian laws stopped First Nations from practising their own spiritual beliefs. But many First Nations continued to practise them despite the laws. Today some Salish are Christians. In recent years, many Salish have returned to their old spiritual beliefs. Others have mixed their traditions with Christianity.

Salish people of all ages participate in ceremonies and celebrations.

Chapter Four

# CELEBRATE!

Each Salish community had its own spiritual beliefs and rituals. Spirit dancing was an important ritual in Coast Salish communities. Special spiritual leaders called shamans helped guide people. They treated the sick. Most shamans were men, but women could also be shamans.

Starting in the 1800s, European **missionaries** visited the Salish. They wanted the Salish to become Christians. Canadian laws stopped First Nations from practising their own spiritual beliefs. But many First Nations continued to practise them despite the laws. Today some Salish are Christians. In recent years, many Salish have returned to their old spiritual beliefs. Others have mixed their traditions with Christianity.

Salish people of all ages participate in ceremonies and celebrations.

16

**SAY IT**

**slhá:lí** (shlayl-LEE): woman

A Salish dancer competes in a powwow.

18

# REASONS TO CELEBRATE

Salish communities celebrated with special ceremonies. Teenagers went on vision quests to get ready to become adults. Young people would go alone into the mountains. They bathed daily in cold rivers. They trained to make contact with a spirit. The spirit helper would guide that person throughout his or her life.

A Salish family might host a **potlatch** to celebrate a marriage, birth, coming of age, or death. A potlatch is a huge feast. It can take many years to plan. It might last two or three weeks. People sing and dance in costumes. Each guest gets a gift and food for the journey home. This might be a carved dish, a canoe, or another keepsake. Traditionally, families gained status by giving away many gifts.

Music was used in spiritual and everyday life. People played drums, whistles, and horns. Sometimes people in masks acted out myths. But singing and dancing were most important. Songs and dances helped people remember traditions. They were also used for playing games and soothing children.

Many modern Salish also enjoy music and dancing. They learn and perform traditional songs and dances. Some Salish events are open to the public. This helps teach the public about Salish cultures and traditions.

## INQUIRY QUESTIONS

How is a potlatch similar to your family celebrations? How did Salish people use their environment to create their traditional homes?

# SALISH TERRITORY

Salish territory covers a large area in southwest Canada and northwest United States. Many Salish live along the coast of the Salish Sea and Fraser River. Others live between the Rocky Mountains and Cascade Range. Salish live in cities and towns in British Columbia and the northwestern United States. Some Salish people live on reserves in Canada.

In 2014 the Supreme Court recognized one Salish nation's title to more than 1,700 square kilometres of land in British Columbia. The nation has the right to control development within this territory. This ruling was the first of its kind. Salish communities continue to work for the rights to their historical lands.

Salish drummers play on decorated drums.

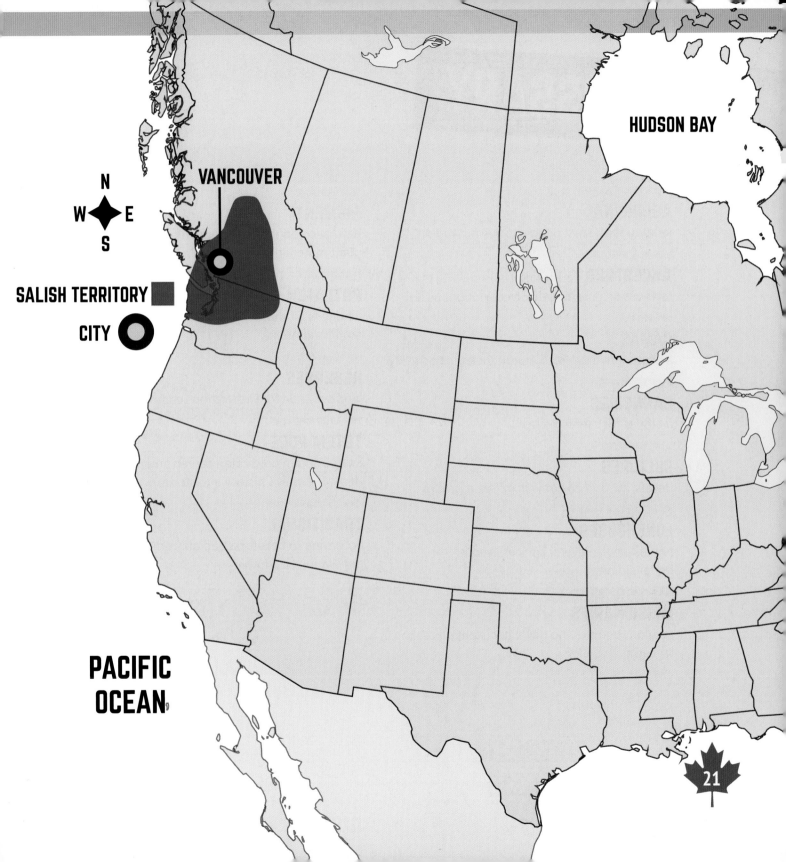

HUDSON BAY

N
W ✦ E
S

VANCOUVER

SALISH TERRITORY ▮

CITY ◉

PACIFIC
OCEAN

21

# GLOSSARY

**ABORIGINAL**
relating to the first people to live in a region

**ANCESTORS**
relatives of a person who lived a long time ago

**CAMAS**
a plant native to North America related to the lily

**CANNERIES**
factories for canning food

**CULTURES**
beliefs, art, and customs of different groups

**LONGHOUSES**
homes where several families lived in one building

**MISSIONARIES**
religious people who travel to distant places to spread their beliefs

**PIGMENT**
natural coloring made from animal or plant material

**POTLATCH**
a huge feast that usually brings together many family members

**RESERVES**
land set aside for First Nations communities

**TOTEM POLE**
a tall wooden pole, often carved and painted to depict a family's history and stories

**TRADITIONAL**
according to beliefs passed on from one generation to another

22

# TO LEARN MORE

## BOOKS

Goldsworthy, Kaite. *British Columbia*. Calgary: Weigl, 2014.

Gurtler, Janet. *Longhouses*. Calgary: Weigl, 2013.

Webster, Christine. *Salish*. Calgary: Weigl, 2011.

## WEBSITES

### CANADA'S FIRST PEOPLE: NORTHWEST COASTAL PEOPLE

**CANADIAN STUDIES PROGRAM CANADIAN HERITAGE**

http://firstpeoplesofcanada.com/

### GATEWAY TO ABORIGINAL HERITAGE

**CANADIAN MUSEUM OF HISTORY**

http://www.historymuseum.ca/cmc/exhibitions/tresors/ethno/ety0105e.shtml

### TERMINOLOGY AND USAGE

**UNIVERSITY OF OTTAWA**

http://www.med.uottawa.ca/sim/data/Aboriginal_Intro_e.htm

# INDEX

# ABOUT THE AUTHOR

M. M. Eboch writes about science, history, and culture for all ages. Her recent non-fiction titles include *Chaco Canyon*, *Living with Dyslexia*, and *The Green Movement*.